Ideal School Supply Company

POLYHEDRA DICE GAMES
For Grades K to 6

Don Balka

POLYHEDRA DICE GAMES
For Grades K to 6

Limited Reproduction Permission: Permission to duplicate these materials is limited to the teacher for whom they are purchased. Reproduction for an entire school or school district is unlawful and strictly prohibited.

The cover photograph shows dice from the collection of Dale Seymour.

Illustrator: Masami Miyamoto
Editor: Lyn Savage

ISBN: 1-56451-062-X
Polyhedra Dice Games, Grades K to 6
© 1993 Ideal School Supply
A Division of Instructional Fair Group, Inc.
3195 Wilson Drive NW, Grand Rapids, MI 49544 • USA
Duke Street, Wisbech, Cambs, PE13 2AE • UK
All Rights Reserved • Printed in USA

FOREWORD

POLYHEDRA DICE GAMES will engage your students in learning mathematical concepts and practicing arithmetic skills through play. In this collection of forty challenging games, polyhedra dice are used to generate random numbers for a variety of activities involving simple counting, numeration, the four basic operations with whole numbers, and for introductory activities involving fractions, decimals, geometric shapes, metric measurement, and coordinate graphing. Some of the games are designed to be played by two to five players; others, by a larger group or an entire class. At least one variation is given for every game, which allows students to play the same game at different levels of skill development or with different goals in mind.

You and your students may discover a need for additional games to teach or reinforce particular mathematical concepts. Encourage your students to think of new games or variations of existing games, for you may find that the most exciting games of all are the ones designed by your students for their classmates. The references listed in the Bibliography may provide some ideas for dice games that can be adapted to specific needs.

I wish you and your students many happy hours of fun and learning with these dice games.

Don Balka

CONTENTS

v

TEACHER NOTES

Game Instructions

The instruction page for each game gives a description of the major mathematical skills involved, the number of players required, the materials needed, a picture of the types of dice used, the rules for play, and variations on the basic game.

The rules for play were designed to be read to the students by you or an aide, or to be read by older students themselves. You may find it helpful to provide one copy of the rules (with variations deleted) for the students to refer to as they play the game.

The following words are used extensively throughout the game rules, and you may wish to review them with your students before they begin the games: *sum, difference, product, quotient.*

In games involving two to five players, it is necessary to determine the order of play. Each set of game rules includes a suggested way of determining the first player; however, you may wish to discuss with the students some ways in which they could decide who plays second, third, and so on. Two methods are suggested: (1) If the first player is determined by rolling the highest (lowest) number, the player rolling the next highest (next lowest) number plays second, and so on. If two players tie, those two players roll the dice again to break the tie. (2) If the players are arranged in a circle, the order of play proceeds in a clockwise direction, beginning with the first player as determined by the rules of the game.

Game Sheets

On the back of each instruction page is a game sheet. Some game sheets contain game boards on which the students will use markers such as beans and chips. To make these game boards more durable, duplicate the page on heavy paper and laminate on both sides, or place the board in a transparent vinyl protector sleeve. Other game sheets are designed to be written on by students, and can be duplicated on regular paper. You might also choose to laminate these game sheets and have students write on them with grease pencils or watercolor markers, making the sheets reusable.

Dice

The games in this collection use one or more of the five polyhedra dice:

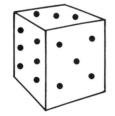

TETRAHEDRON DIE

Faces: 4 equilateral triangles
Possible numbers: 1, 2, 3, 4
To read the number rolled, look at the number which is at the bottom of each face of the cube as it rests on the table. In the figure at the left, the number rolled is 4.

HEXAHEDRON DIE

Faces: 6 squares
Possible numbers: 1, 2, 3, 4, 5, 6
This is the ordinary die which is shaped like a cube or hexahedron. The faces may have numerals or sets of dots to indicate the number rolled.
Read the number on the top face of the die.

OCTAHEDRON DIE

Faces: 8 equilateral triangles
Possible numbers: 1, 2, 3, 4, 5, 6, 7, 8
Read the number on the top face of the die.

DODECAHEDRON DIE

Faces: 12 regular pentagons
Possible numbers: 1, 2, 3, 4, 5, 6, 7, 8, 9, 10, 11, 12
Read the number on the top face of the die.

ICOSAHEDRON DIE

Faces: 20 equilateral triangles
Possible numbers: 0, 1, 2, 3, 4, 5, 6, 7, 8, 9
Each of the digits 0 through 9 appears twice on this die, making it possible to generate random digits. Read the number on the top face of the die.

Sets of polyhedra dice are available from Creative Publications. You may also make your own polyhedra dice by using the patterns provided.

Alternatives to Using Dice

If you do not have enough polyhedra dice for certain activities, you could use one of these alternate ways to generate the numbers needed to play the games: (1) Use spinners numbered with the numbers on the required dice. (2) Fill a bag with cubes or ping-pong balls on which you have written the numbers required. Draw one cube or ball at a time from the bag. Replace it and shake the bag before drawing again.

The following table shows the numbers for each of the five polyhedra dice.

Die	Numbers for Spinner, Balls, or Cubes
Tetrahedron	1, 2, 3, 4
Hexahedron	1, 2, 3, 4, 5, 6
Octahedron	1, 2, 3, 4, 5, 6, 7, 8
Dodecahedron	1, 2, 3, 4, 5, 6, 7, 8, 9, 10, 11, 12
Icosahedron	0, 1, 2, 3, 4, 5, 6, 7, 8, 9

PATTERNS FOR FIVE REGULAR POLYHEDRA DICE

REGULAR TETRAHEDRON

Duplicate on tagboard. Cut on solid lines. Fold on dotted lines. Tape or glue together. Number faces 1 through 4.

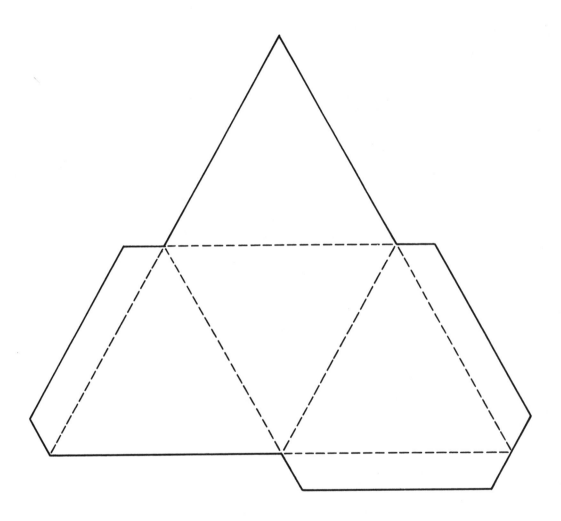

REGULAR HEXAHEDRON

Duplicate on tagboard. Cut on solid lines. Fold on dotted lines. Tape or glue together.
Number faces 1 through 6.

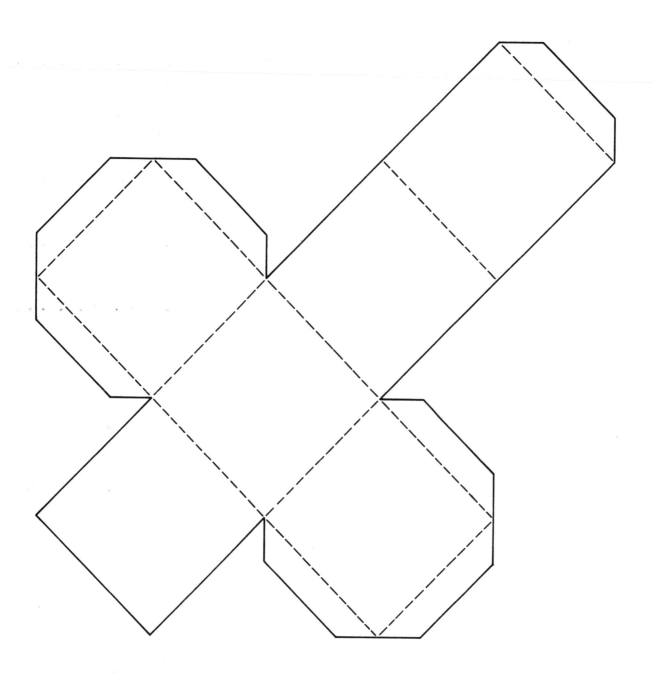

x

REGULAR OCTAHEDRON

Duplicate on tagboard. Cut on solid lines. Fold on dotted lines. Tape or glue together. Number faces 1 through 8.

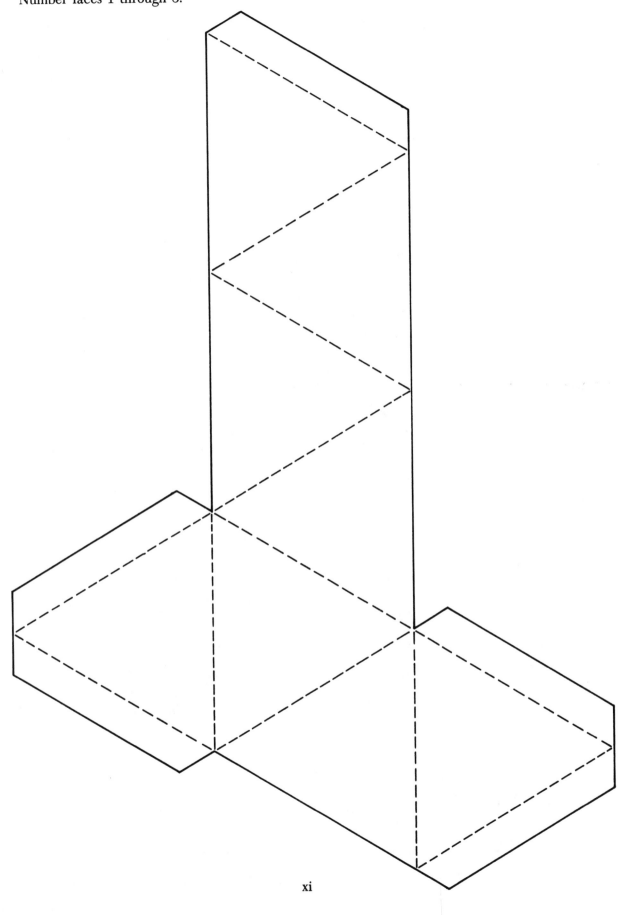

xi

REGULAR DODECAHEDRON

Duplicate on tagboard. Cut on solid lines. Fold on dotted lines. Tape or glue together. Number faces 1 through 12.

xii

REGULAR ICOSAHEDRON

Duplicate on tagboard. Cut on solid lines. Fold on dotted lines. Tape or glue together. Number faces 0 through 9, using each number twice.

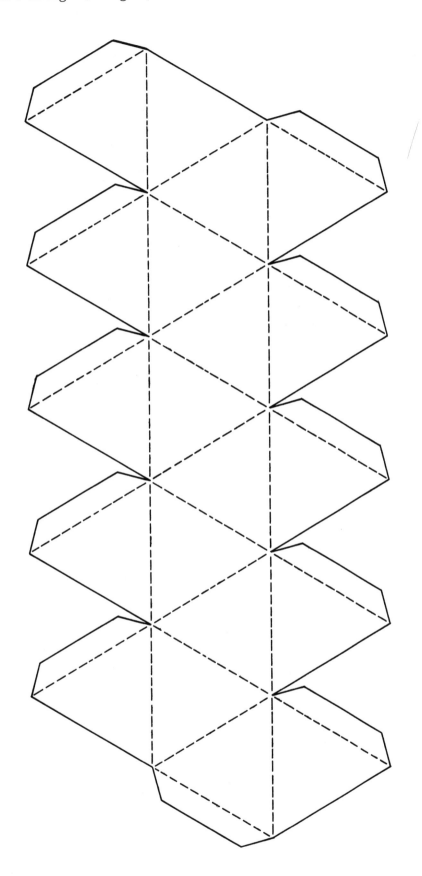

xiii

BIBLIOGRAPHY

The Diagram Group. *The Way to Play: The Illustrated Encyclopedia of the Games of the World.* New York: Paddington Press, Ltd., 1975.

Frey, Skip. *Complete Book of Dice Games.* New York: Hart Publishing Co., Inc., 1975.

Ore, Oystein. *Cardano, the Gambling Scholar.* New York: Dover Publications, n.d.

Scarne, John. *Scarne on Dice.* Harrisburg, Pennsylvania: Stackpole Books, 1974.

Silvey, Linda. *Polyhedra Dice Games for Grades 5 to 10.* Palo Alto, California: Creative Publications, Inc., 1978.

WIN ONE

MATH SKILL

Matching numerals with number words

NUMBER OF PLAYERS

2

MATERIALS

1 icosahedron die
Game sheet 1
1 marker per player

HOW TO PLAY

Put your markers on *START*.

Roll the die to see who begins. Whoever rolls the higher number starts.

Take turns rolling the die. Move your marker forward to the *first* space that contains the word-form of the number that you rolled.

If you cannot move forward, you lose that turn.

You may share a space with another player.

The first player to land on the *LAST ONE* is the winner. To land on the *LAST ONE* you must roll a 1.

VARIATION

Two players may not share the same space. If a player must land on an occupied space to complete a move, the turn is lost.

GAME SHEET 1

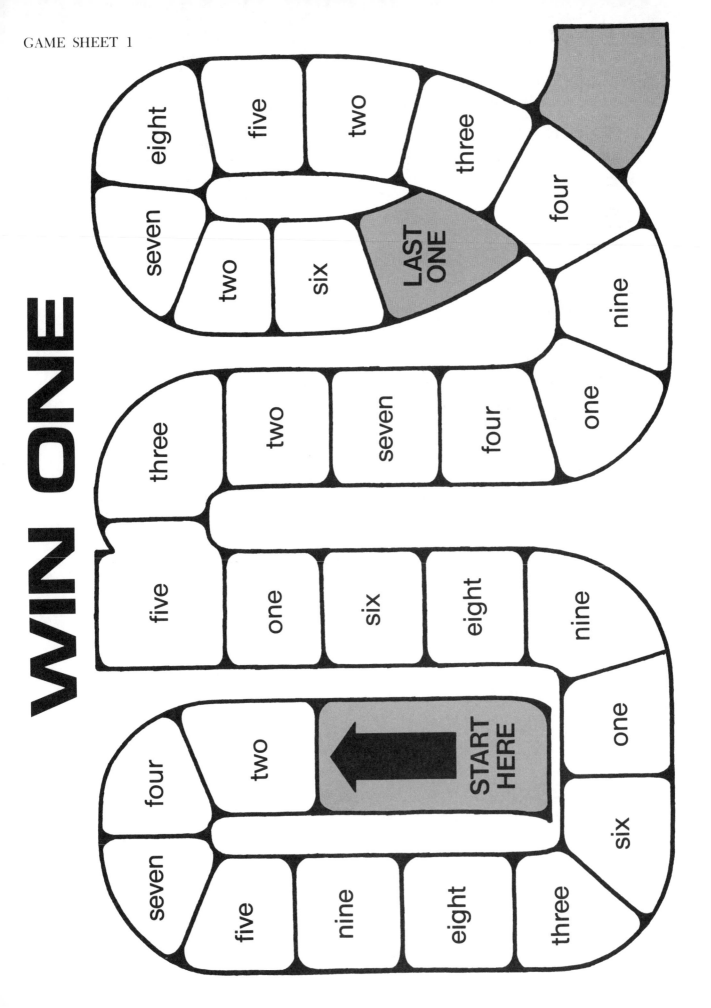

MATCH ME

MATH SKILLS

Identifying the number of elements in a set
Matching a given number with a set containing that number of elements

NUMBER OF PLAYERS

2

MATERIALS

1 icosahedron die
Game sheet 2
1 marker per player

HOW TO PLAY

Put your markers on *START*.

Roll the die to see who begins. Whoever rolls the lower number starts.

Take turns rolling the die. Move your marker forward to the *first* space that contains the same number of shapes as the number you rolled.

If you cannot move forward, you lose that turn.

You may share a space with another player.

The first player to land on *FINISH* is the winner. To land on *FINISH* you must roll a 1.

VARIATION

Two players may not share the same space. If a player must land on an occupied space to complete a move, the turn is lost.

GAME SHEET 2

MATCH ME

FINISH

START

POLYHEDRA DICE GAMES For Grades K to 6   © 1993 Ideal School Supply Company

IN THE DOGHOUSE

MATH SKILLS

  Number recognition and counting

NUMBER OF PLAYERS

  2

MATERIALS

  1 octahedron die
  Game sheet 3
  1 marker per player

HOW TO PLAY

  Put your markers on the *DOGHOUSE*.

  Roll the die to see who begins. Whoever rolls the higher number starts.

  Take turns rolling the die. Move your marker the number of spaces shown by the die.

  If you land on a space that has a dog in it, you must return your marker to the *DOGHOUSE* and start again.

  You may share a space with another player.

  The first player to land on or pass the *BONE* is the winner. The exact number does not have to be rolled.

VARIATION

  To land on the *BONE*, a player must roll a number equal to the number of spaces left to move.

IN THE DOGHOUSE

HOT DOG!

MATH SKILL
   Ordering the numbers 0 through 9

NUMBER OF PLAYERS
   2

MATERIALS

   1 icosahedron die
   Game sheet 4 (duplicate 1 sheet per player)
   Scissors

HOW TO PLAY
   The object of the game is to arrange all the pieces of your hot dog in order from
   0 through 9.

   Cut the pieces of your hot dog apart.

   Choose any piece of your hot dog and place it face up in front of you. Keep the other
   pieces nearby.

   Roll the die to see who begins. Whoever rolls the lower number starts.

   Take turns rolling the die. Try to match the number you roll to one of your hot dog
   pieces. If you make a match and that number comes just before or just after a piece
   already played, you may add that piece to your hot dog. For example, if pieces 3 and
   4 have been played, you must roll a 2 or a 5 to add another piece to your hot dog.
   If you cannot add a piece to your hot dog or if you roll the number of a piece already
   played, the turn is lost.

   The first player to get all 10 pieces in order is the winner.

VARIATION
   Duplicate 2 game sheets per player. Renumber the pieces 0 through 18. The players
   take turns rolling a pair of icosahedra dice. They are to find the sum of the 2 numbers
   rolled and match that sum to the corresponding piece of their hot dog. The first player
   to get all the pieces in order from 0 through 18 is the winner.

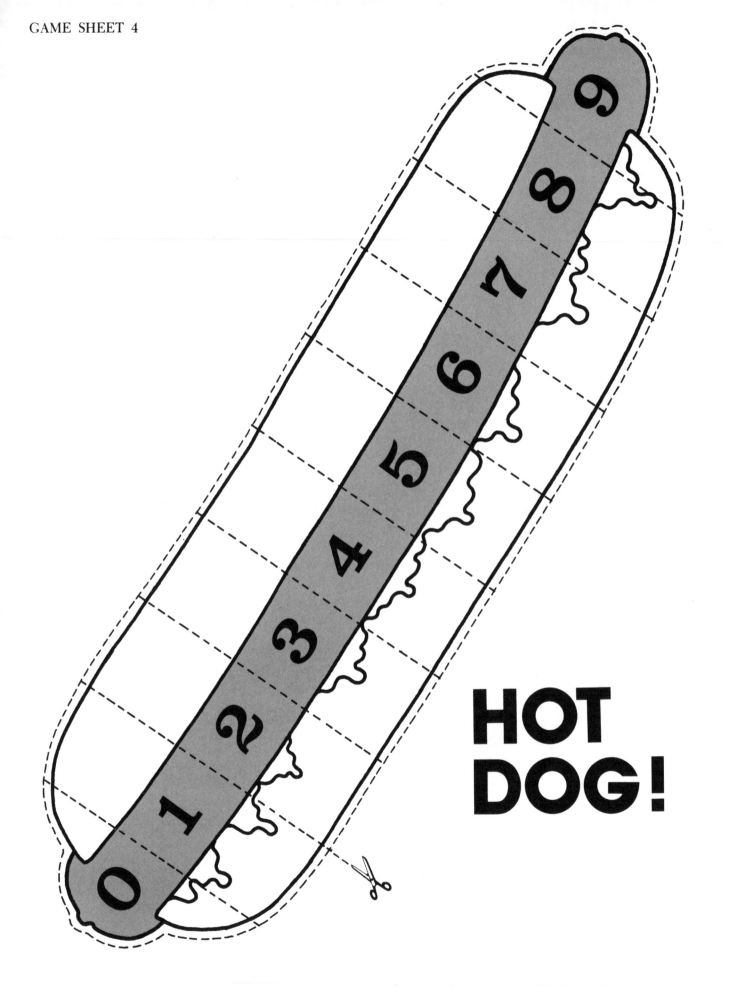

HOT DOG!

ODDBALL

MATH SKILL
Identifying the odd and even numbers through 12

NUMBER OF PLAYERS
2

MATERIALS

1 dodecahedron die
Game sheet 5
1 marker per player

HOW TO PLAY
Roll the die to see who begins. Whoever rolls the higher number starts, and chooses to play the *ODD* track or the *EVEN* track. The other player plays the remaining track.

Take turns rolling the die. If you are playing the *ODD* track and you roll an odd number, you may move your marker forward 1 space. You may not move if you roll an even number. If you are playing the *EVEN* track and you roll an even number, you may move your marker forward 1 space. You may not move if you roll an odd number.

The first player to land on the *ODDBALL* is the winner.

VARIATION
Play the game in the same way, except when the *ODD*-track player rolls an even number, the *EVEN*-track player may move 1 space. When the *EVEN*-track player rolls an odd number, the *ODD*-track player may move 1 space. The first player to win 2 out of 3 games is the winner.

EVEN START

ODD START

ODDBALL

ADAM UP

MATH SKILL
  Basic addition facts for sums through 12

NUMBER OF PLAYERS
  2 to 4

MATERIALS

  1 dodecahedron die
  Game sheet 6
  Scissors
  Pencil
  Scratch paper

HOW TO PLAY
  Cut the ADAM UP cards apart and place them face up on the table or desk.

  Decide how many turns each player will have in the game. All players have the same number of turns.

  Roll the die to see who begins. Whoever rolls the lowest number starts.

  Take turns rolling the die. After each roll, pick up any pair of cards whose sum is the number you rolled. Continue to roll the die and pick up pairs of cards until you roll a number for which no pair of addends remains. Then count the number of cards you picked up and record that number on scratch paper.

  Replace all the cards face up for the next player.

  The game ends after all the players have had the number of turns decided before the game.

  Add to find out how many cards you collected in all. The player who collects the most cards is the winner.

VARIATION
  The player who collects the most cards after a given time period (regardless of turns) is the winner.

ADAM UP

POLYHEDRA DICE GAMES For Grades K to 6   © 1993 Ideal School Supply Company

EGGHEAD

MATH SKILL
Basic addition facts for sums through 12

NUMBER OF PLAYERS
2

MATERIALS

2 hexahedra dice
Game sheet 7
1 small marker per player

HOW TO PLAY
The object of the game is to move your markers from egg to egg by finding sums.

Put your markers on *START*.

Roll the dice to see who begins. Whoever rolls the greater sum starts.

Roll the dice. If the sum of the 2 numbers you roll is in the first egg, move your marker to that egg; otherwise, stay on *START*. Take turns rolling the dice. After each roll, try to move your marker to the next egg by finding the sum of the numbers you roll. You may only move your marker if the sum of the numbers you roll is in the next egg.

Continue the game until a player lands on the *EGGHEAD*.

The first player to land on the *EGGHEAD* is the winner.

VARIATIONS
Change the sums in the eggs and have the players use other polyhedra dice.

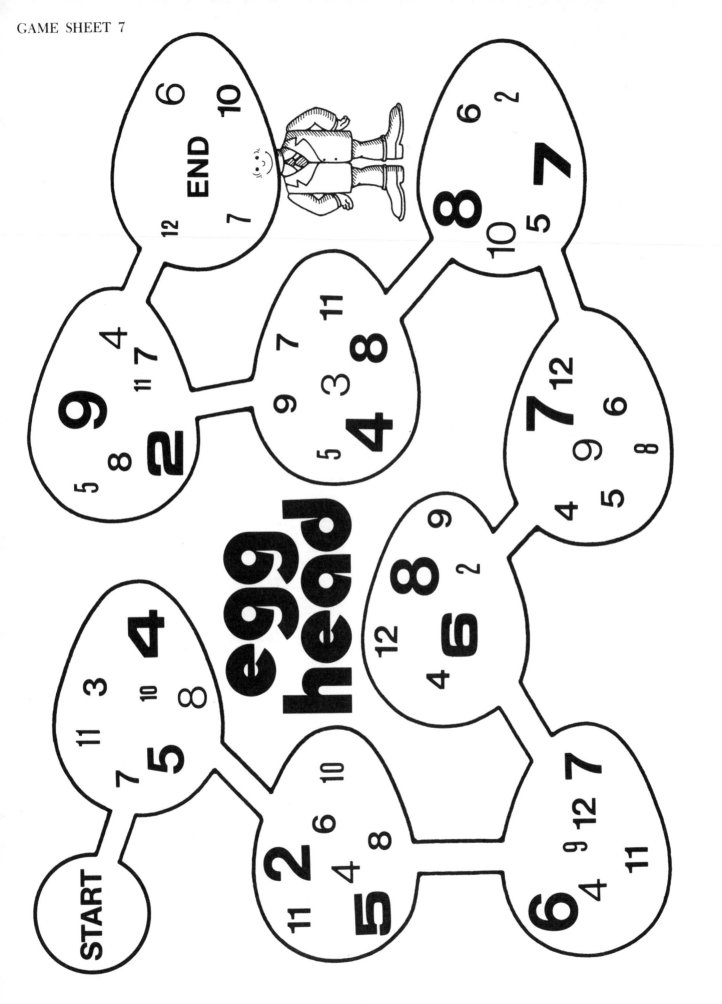

DICE WAR

MATH SKILLS
Basic addition facts for sums through 12
Comparing sums (using inequalities)

NUMBER OF PLAYERS
2 to 5

MATERIALS

2 hexahedra dice per player
Game sheet 8
1 pencil

HOW TO PLAY
The object of the game is to earn 10 points.

Each player rolls 2 dice. Whoever rolls the greatest sum acts as scorekeeper for all players. The scorekeeper records each player's points in the correct column on the game sheet, and writes the running total for each column.

All players roll the dice at the same time. The player who rolls the greatest sum earns one point.

If there is a tie between 2 or more players, all the players roll their dice again. The winner of that roll receives 2 points.

The first player to earn 10 points is the winner.

VARIATIONS
The player who rolls the greatest difference, greatest product, least sum, least difference, or least product earns the point.

Use 3 dice per player. The player who rolls the greatest sum, greatest product, least sum, or least product is the winner.

DICE WAR

PLAYERS' NAMES					

QUAD

MATH SKILL
Basic addition facts for sums through 18

NUMBER OF PLAYERS
2 to 4

MATERIALS

2 icosahedra dice
Game sheet 9
10 small markers per player
Scissors

HOW TO PLAY
The object of the game is to get 4 markers in a row in any direction—horizontal, vertical, or diagonal.

Cut the QUAD cards apart. Each player chooses 1 card for the first game.

The player whose last name begins with the letter closest to M starts.

Take turns rolling the dice. Find the sum of the 2 numbers you rolled; then place a marker on the space containing that sum.

If the sum you roll is not on your card, you lose that turn.

The first player to get 4 markers in a row in any direction is the winner.

Exchange QUAD cards and play again in the same way.

VARIATIONS
Provide each player with a blank QUAD card. Tell them to write any number from 0 through 18 in each space. They may use the same number more than once. Then have them play the game as suggested above.

GAME SHEET 9

QUAD			
3	12	17	16
13	10	4	8
9	5	2	1
5	8	14	15

QUAD			
7	10	16	18
12	1	14	15
2	11	13	3
4	6	8	17

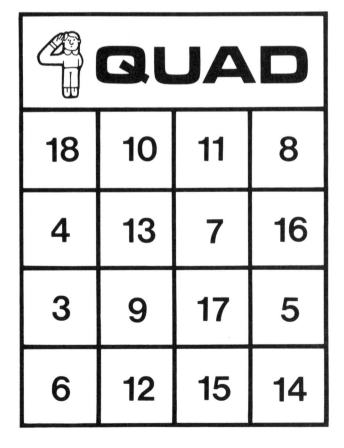

QUAD			
18	10	11	8
4	13	7	16
3	9	17	5
6	12	15	14

QUAD			
16	7	17	15
5	1	12	6
8	18	9	4
13	11	14	10

SINGLE OUT

MATH SKILL
    Addition of three 1-digit addends for sums through 18, with and without regrouping

NUMBER OF PLAYERS
    A class or small group

MATERIALS

    1 hexahedron die
    Game sheet 10 (duplicate 1 sheet per player)
    1 pencil per player

HOW TO PLAY
    The object of the game is to get the highest score.

    The teacher (or a student designated by the teacher) rolls the die and calls out the number.

    Write the number rolled in any of the 9 squares of your *GAME 1* grid.

    Continue the game until all the squares of the grid are filled.

    Find the sum of the 3 numbers in each row and write it beside the row. Find the sum of the 3 numbers in each column and write it below the column.

    Look at your 6 sums and cross out the sums that only appear once.

    Add up the remaining sums to find your score.

    The player with the highest score wins.

    Play games 2, 3, and 4 in the same way.

    Example:

6	2	1	~~9~~
1	3	6	~~10~~
1	2	1	~~4~~
8	~~7~~	8	

SCORE: 16

VARIATION
    Use a tetrahedron die for lesser sums, or an octahedron or icosahedron die for greater sums.

SINGLE OUT

_____
NAME

GAME 1

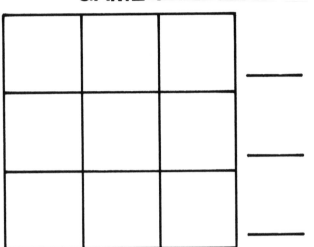

SCORE _____

GAME 2

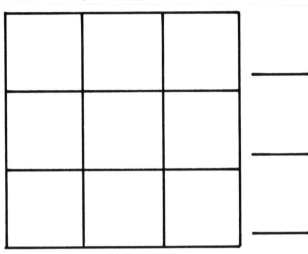

SCORE _____

GAME 3

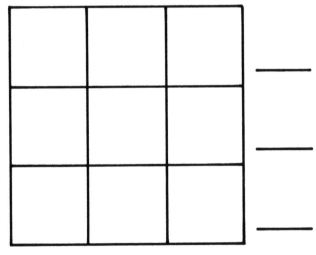

SCORE _____

GAME 4

SCORE _____

BOXING MATCH

MATH SKILL

Addition of 1- and 2-digit addends for sums through 20

NUMBER OF PLAYERS

2

MATERIALS

2 hexahedra dice
Game sheet 11 (duplicate 1 sheet and cut in half)
2 pencils

HOW TO PLAY

The object of the game is to correctly complete the equations.

Roll the dice to see who begins. Whoever rolls the lesser sum plays first.

Take turns rolling the dice. Find the sum of the 2 numbers you rolled, and place it in one of the boxes on your game sheet. Continue in this way until you have placed 4 numbers on your game sheet. For each turn after that, you may choose to place either the sum of the numbers rolled, or just one of the numbers rolled, in one of the boxes on your game sheet. For example, if you already filled in 4 or more boxes on your game sheet, and you roll a 5 and a 2, you may choose to put a 7, a 5, or a 2 in one of the boxes on your game sheet.

If you cannot place a number on your game sheet without making an incorrect equation, you lose that turn.

The first player to correctly complete all the equations is the winner.

VARIATION

Use 2 octahedra dice.

BOXING MATCH

NAME _____

□ + □ = 7

□ + □ = 12

□ + □ = 16

□ + □ + □ = 15

□ + □ + □ = 20

BOXING MATCH

NAME _____

□ + □ = 7

□ + □ = 12

□ + □ = 16

□ + □ + □ = 15

□ + □ + □ = 20

LOWEST IS BEST

MATH SKILLS
Basic addition facts for sums through 18
Column addition of 1- and 2-digit addends, with and without regrouping

NUMBER OF PLAYERS
2

MATERIALS

2 icosahedra dice
Game sheet 12
24 markers per player
Pencil
Scratch paper

HOW TO PLAY
Roll the dice to see who begins. Whoever rolls the lesser sum starts.

Take turns rolling the dice. Find the sum of the 2 numbers you rolled. Use a marker to cover that sum on your side of the game sheet.

If you have already covered a sum, you lose that turn.

Each time you have a turn, set aside 1 marker. This will help you remember how many turns you have had.

Keep playing until both players have had 12 turns.

Find the sum of all your *uncovered* numbers.

The player with the lesser sum is the winner.

VARIATIONS
Have the players find the sum of all the *covered* numbers. The player with the greater sum is the winner.

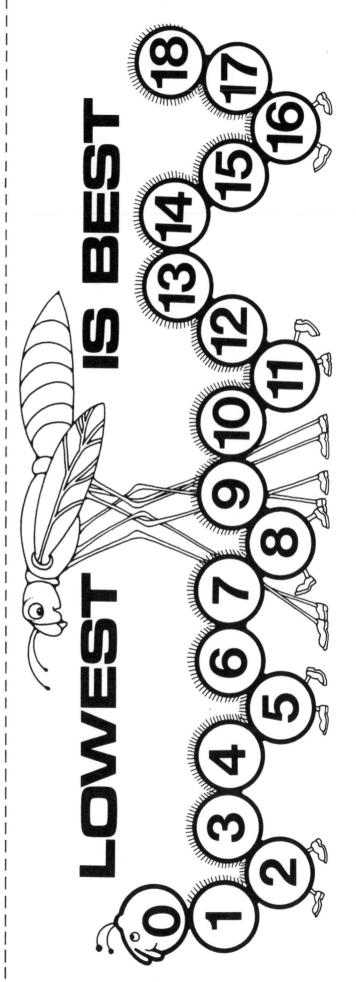

LOWEST IS BEST

IS BEST

LOWEST

GRAND TOTAL

MATH SKILL
   Addition of 1- and 2-digit addends, with and without regrouping

NUMBER OF PLAYERS
   2 to 4

MATERIALS

   2 tetrahedra dice
   Game sheet 13
   1 marker per player
   Pencils
   Scratch paper

HOW TO PLAY
   The object of the game is to move your marker to or past *100*.

   Roll the dice to see who begins. The player who rolls the greatest sum plays first.

   All players start with their markers on *1*.

   Take turns rolling the dice. Add the sum of the numbers you rolled to the number of the space your marker is on. Move your marker to the answer.

   If your marker would land on a space already occupied by another marker, you lose that turn.

   The first player to land on or pass *100* is the winner.

VARIATIONS
   Use 1 octahedron die, 1 dodecahedron die, or 1 icosahedron die.

   When you land on a space, write your initials on it. If your marker would land on a space with someone's initials already on it, you lose your turn. The game ends when one player lands on or passes *100*. The player who has the most initials on the game board wins the game.

POLYHEDRA DICE GAMES For Grades K to 6   © 1993 Ideal School Supply Company

GRAND TOTAL

1	2	3	4	5	6	7	8	9	10
11	12	13	14	15	16	17	18	19	20
21	22	23	24	25	26	27	28	29	30
31	32	33	34	35	36	37	38	39	40
41	42	43	44	45	46	47	48	49	50
51	52	53	54	55	56	57	58	59	60
61	62	63	64	65	66	67	68	69	70
71	72	73	74	75	76	77	78	79	80
81	82	83	84	85	86	87	88	89	90
91	92	93	94	95	96	97	98	99	100

SUMMIT

MATH SKILL
   Addition of two 3-digit addends

NUMBER OF PLAYERS
   A class or small group

MATERIALS

   1 octahedron die
   Game sheet 14 (duplicate 1 sheet per player)
   1 pencil per player

HOW TO PLAY
   The object of the game is to get the greatest sum.

   The teacher (or a student designated by the teacher) rolls the die and calls out the number.

   Write that number in any of the 6 boxes in *GAME 1*.

   Continue the game until all 6 boxes are filled.

   You now have two 3-digit numbers written. Find their sum and write it in the space provided.

   The player who gets the greatest sum wins.

   Play games 2, 3, and 4 in the same way.

VARIATIONS
   Use an icosahedron die, or a hexahedron (ordinary) die.

   The object of the game is to get the least sum.

GAME SHEET 14

NAME _____

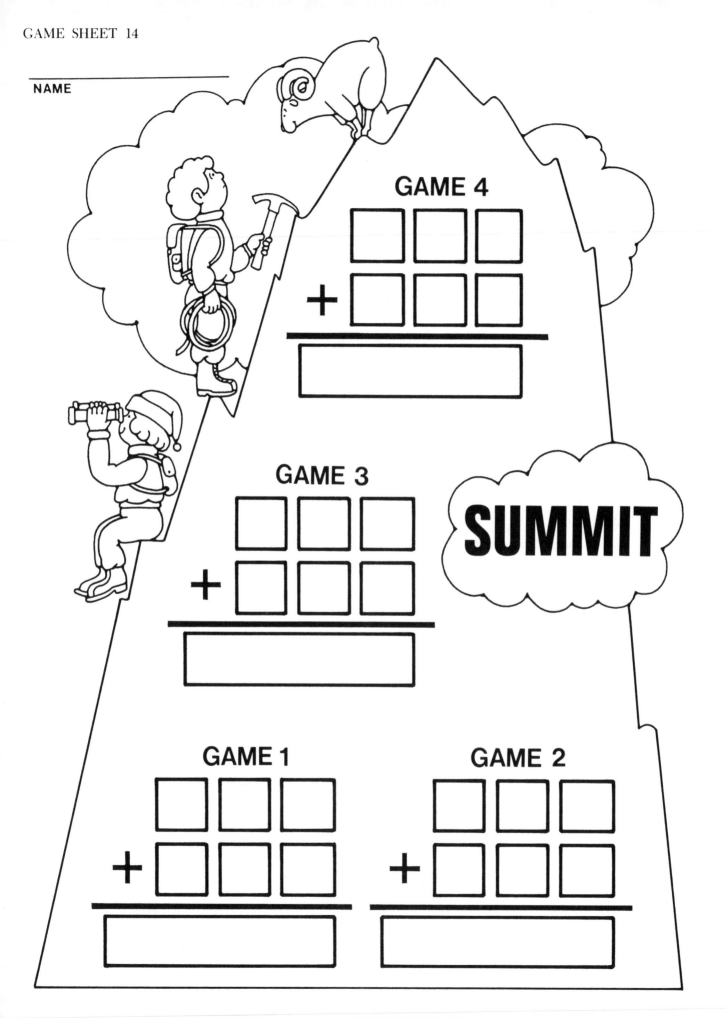

GAME 4

$+$

GAME 3

$+$

SUMMIT

GAME 1

$+$

GAME 2

$+$

POLYHEDRA DICE GAMES For Grades K to 6   © 1993 Ideal School Supply Company

ROLLER COASTER

MATH SKILL
Addition of positive and negative integers

NUMBER OF PLAYERS
2

MATERIALS

1 octahedron die
Game sheet 15
1 marker per player
1 pencil per player

HOW TO PLAY
The object of the game is to get the higher total score.

Roll the die to see who begins. Whoever gets the higher odd number plays first.

Take turns rolling the die. Move your marker forward the number of spaces shown on the die. Add the number you land on to the number you rolled, and state the sum. Write the sum on your *SCOREBOARD*.

Two markers may occupy the same space on the *ROLLER COASTER*.

The game ends when one player lands on or passes the *END*.

Add up all the numbers on your *SCOREBOARD*.

The player who gets the higher total wins.

VARIATION
The player with the lower total wins.

GAME SHEET 15

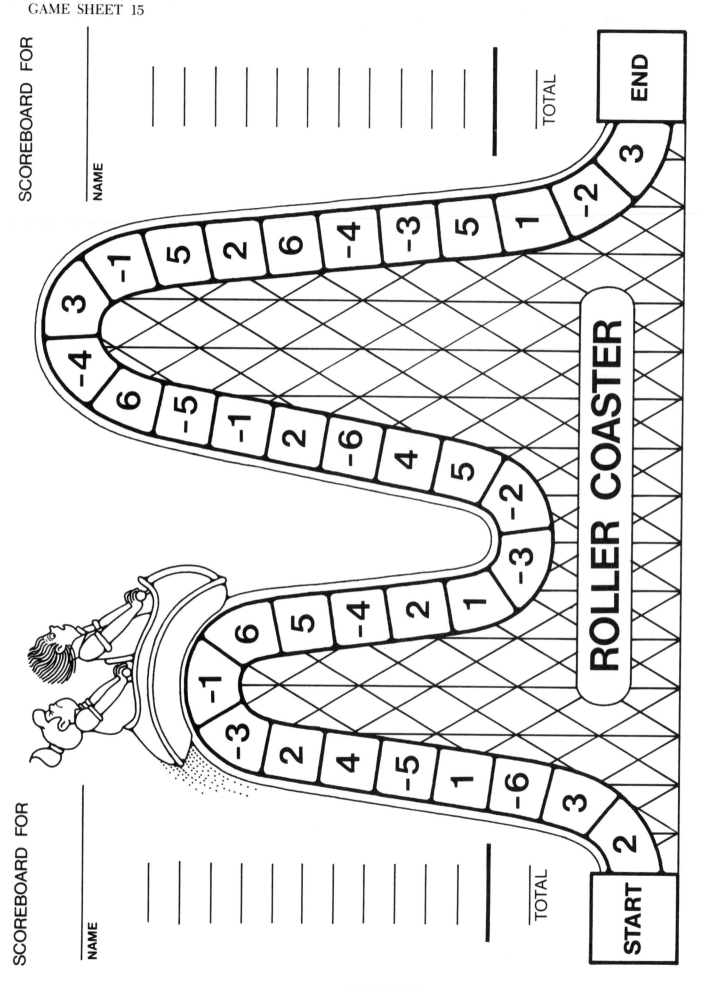

SCOREBOARD FOR

NAME

TOTAL

SCOREBOARD FOR

NAME

TOTAL

END

ROLLER COASTER

START

3

-2

1

5

-3

6

-4

2

5

-1

3

-4

6

-5

-1

2

-6

4

5

-2

-3

1

2

-4

5

6

-1

-3

2

4

-5

1

-6

3

2

DIFFY

MATH SKILL
Basic subtraction facts related to sums through 18

NUMBER OF PLAYERS
2 to 4

MATERIALS

1 icosahedron die
Game sheet 16
10 markers per player
Scissors

HOW TO PLAY
The object of the game is to get 4 markers in a row in any direction—horizontal, vertical, or diagonal.

Cut the DIFFY cards apart. Each player chooses 1 card for the first game.

The player whose first name begins with the letter closest to A starts.

Take turns rolling the die. Cover one subtraction problem on your card that has an answer equal to the number you rolled.

If your card does not have a subtraction problem with an answer equal to the number you roll, you lose that turn.

The first player to get 4 markers in a row in any direction is the winner.

Exchange DIFFY cards and play again in the same way.

VARIATION
The first player to cover all spaces on the card is the winner. (This variation may take several minutes to play.)

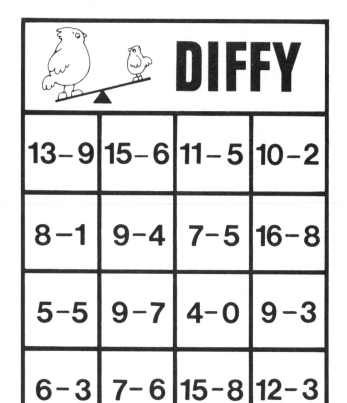

DIFFY

13 − 9	15 − 6	11 − 5	10 − 2
8 − 1	9 − 4	7 − 5	16 − 8
5 − 5	9 − 7	4 − 0	9 − 3
6 − 3	7 − 6	15 − 8	12 − 3

DIFFY

5 − 3	13 − 4	12 − 7	10 − 9
8 − 5	8 − 4	17 − 9	8 − 6
13 − 6	6 − 6	12 − 6	7 − 0
5 − 4	16 − 7	5 − 1	11 − 3

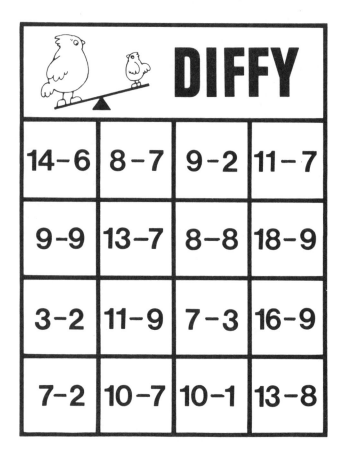

DIFFY

14 − 6	8 − 7	9 − 2	11 − 7
9 − 9	13 − 7	8 − 8	18 − 9
3 − 2	11 − 9	7 − 3	16 − 9
7 − 2	10 − 7	10 − 1	13 − 8

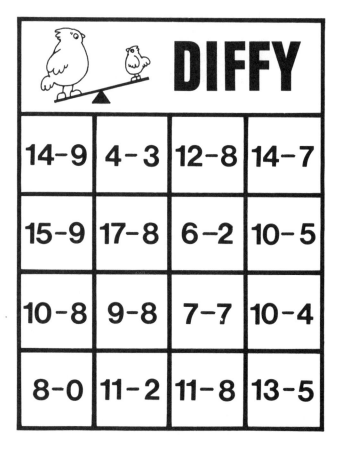

DIFFY

14 − 9	4 − 3	12 − 8	14 − 7
15 − 9	17 − 8	6 − 2	10 − 5
10 − 8	9 − 8	7 − 7	10 − 4
8 − 0	11 − 2	11 − 8	13 − 5

SUBMARINE

MATH SKILL
Basic subtraction facts related to sums through 18

NUMBER OF PLAYERS
2 to 4

MATERIALS

1 icosahedron die
Game sheet 17 (duplicate 1 sheet per player)
1 pencil per player

HOW TO PLAY
The object of the game is to cross out as many numbers as possible on your *SUBMARINE*.

Roll the die to see who begins. Whoever rolls the lowest number plays first.

Take turns rolling the die. Cross out 2 numbers whose difference is equal to the number rolled, and state the subtraction problem you have used. For example, if you roll an 8, you might cross out 12 and 4, saying "12 – 4 = 8," or you might cross out 18 and 10, saying "18 – 10 = 8."

If you roll a zero, you lose that turn.

If you state an incorrect subtraction equation, you lose that turn.

When you roll a number for which you cannot find 2 numbers to cross out, stop playing and total your score. All players continue rolling the die until they must stop playing.

Your score is the sum of the numbers you have crossed out.

When all players have finished their games and have found their scores, the player with the highest score is declared the winner.

VARIATION
Your score is the sum of the numbers you have *not* crossed out. The player with the lowest score wins.

NAME_____

SUBMARINE

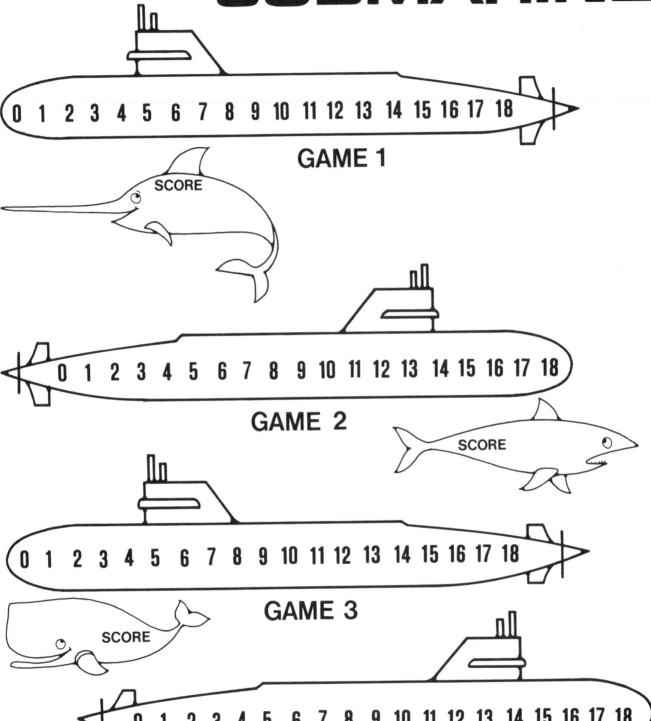

GAME 1

SCORE

GAME 2

SCORE

GAME 3

SCORE

GAME 4

SCORE

COUNT DOWN

MATH SKILL
  Subtraction of 1-, 2-, and 3-digit numbers

NUMBER OF PLAYERS
  2 to 4

MATERIALS

  3 icosahedra dice
  Game sheet 18 (duplicate 1 sheet per player)
  1 pencil per player

HOW TO PLAY

  The object of the game is to reach zero.

  Roll the dice to see who begins. The player with the least sum plays first.

  Take turns rolling all 3 dice. From the 3 numbers rolled, you may make either a 1-digit, 2-digit, or 3-digit number. Write that number below the *1000* in *ROCKET 1* on your game sheet, and subtract. On your next turn, you roll the dice again, make another number, and subtract it from your first answer.

  If you cannot subtract a particular number, you lose that turn.

  The first player to reach an answer of zero is the winner.

  Play again using the other rockets on your game sheet.

  Example:

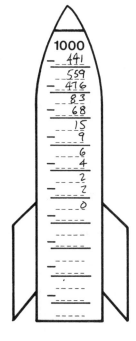

VARIATION

  Use 3 octahedra dice or 3 hexahedra (ordinary) dice.

NAME

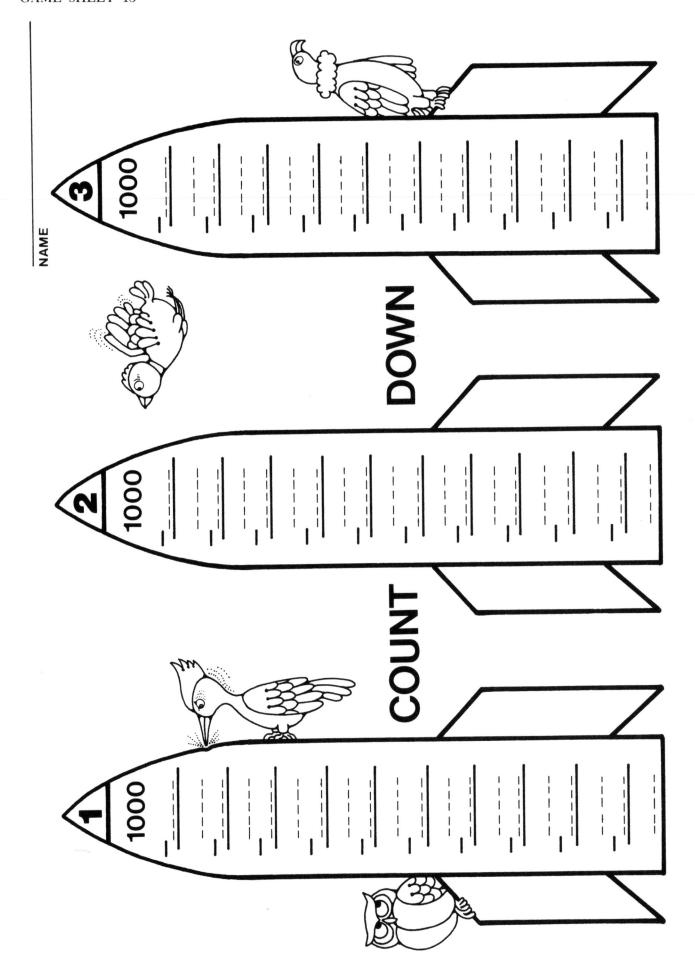

3   1000

DOWN

2   1000

COUNT

1   1000

CRISSCROSS

MATH SKILL

Basic multiplication facts for products through 81

NUMBER OF PLAYERS

2 to 4

MATERIALS

2 icosahedra dice
Game sheet 19
4 markers per player
Scissors

HOW TO PLAY

The object of the game is to place 4 markers on your CRISSCROSS card.

Cut the CRISSCROSS cards apart. Each player chooses 1 card for the first game.

The player whose last name begins with the letter closest to Z starts.

Take turns rolling the dice. Find the product of the 2 numbers you rolled; then place a marker on the space containing that product.

If the product you roll is not on your card, you lose that turn.

The first player to place 4 markers on a card is the winner.

Exchange CRISSCROSS cards and play again in the same way.

VARIATION

The first player to get 4 markers in a row in any direction is the winner. (This variation may take several minutes to play.)

criss cross

6	16	49	42
9	0	21	24
2	32	25	72
63	40	18	15

criss cross

81	3	20	56
16	48	18	54
0	27	45	9
49	24	28	8

criss cross

16	5	63	72
12	20	14	18
24	30	48	0
10	56	15	81

criss cross

4	36	18	0
16	24	35	15
27	7	32	28
54	12	64	72

BASEBALL

MATH SKILL
Basic multiplication facts for products through 81

NUMBER OF PLAYERS
2 players or 2 teams

MATERIALS

2 icosahedra dice
Game sheet 20
4 markers
Pencil

HOW TO PLAY
The object of the game is to score the most runs in 6 innings of play.

Each team (player) rolls the dice to see who begins play. The team that rolls the greater product is the A's team and comes to bat first.

Roll the dice and use the *BATTING CHART* to see if you have hit a single, double, triple, or homerun, or if you are out. Continue rolling the dice until your team has made 3 outs.

All players on base run the number of bases that the batter hits and runs.

If you roll doubles, you may either use the chart for your hit, or you may roll the dice again.

An incorrect answer is an automatic out.

The team with the higher score at the end of 6 full innings is the winner.

VARIATION
Use 2 dodecahedra dice for products through 144, and change the *BATTING CHART* accordingly.

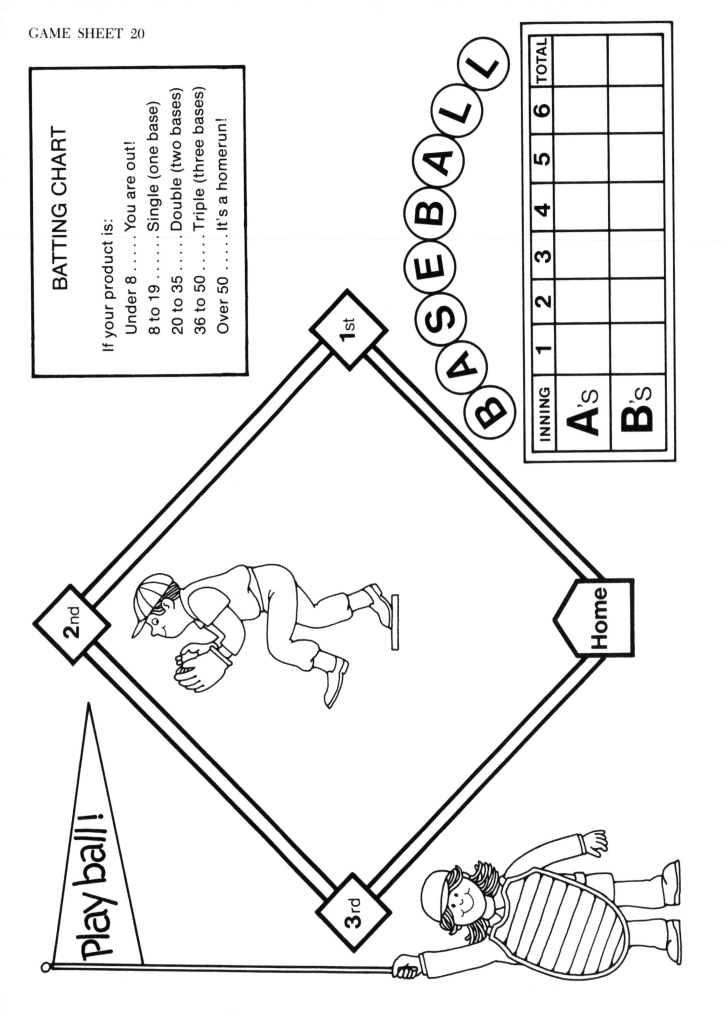

BATTING CHART

If your product is:

Under 8 . . . . . . You are out!
8 to 19 . . . . . . Single (one base)
20 to 35 . . . . . . Double (two bases)
36 to 50 . . . . . . Triple (three bases)
Over 50 . . . . . . It's a homerun!

BASEBALL

INNING	1	2	3	4	5	6	TOTAL
A's							
B's							

1st

2nd

Home

3rd

Play ball!

THE BIG TABLE

MATH SKILL
  Basic multiplication facts for products through 144

NUMBER OF PLAYERS
  2 to 5

MATERIALS

  2 dodecahedra dice
  Game sheet 21
  1 pencil per player

HOW TO PLAY
  The object of the game is to complete a row of 6 products in any direction—horizontal, vertical, or diagonal.

  Roll the dice to see who begins. The player who gets the greatest product plays first.

  Take turns rolling the dice. Find 1 space on the table which corresponds to the numbers you rolled, and write the product of the 2 numbers in that space. For example, if you roll 5 and 7, write the answer 35 either in the space in row 5 column 7, *or* in the space in row 7 column 5.

  If you cannot find an empty space for the product of the 2 numbers you roll, you lose that turn.

  If a player gives an incorrect product, you may challenge that player. If you can give the correct product, you may write it in the proper space.

  The first player to complete any row of 6 products is the winner.

VARIATION
  Use 2 octahedra dice and reduce the table to an 8 × 8 grid.

X	1	2	3	4	5	6	7	8	9	10	11	12
1												
2												
3												
4												
5												
6												
7												
8												
9												
10												
11												
12												

THE BIG TABLE

BIG GAME HUNT

MATH SKILLS
Multiplication of 1- and 2-digit numbers for products through 144
Equations and inequalities

NUMBER OF PLAYERS
2

MATERIALS

2 hexahedra dice
Game sheet 22 (duplicate 1 sheet and cut in half)
2 pencils

HOW TO PLAY
The object of the game is to correctly complete the number sentences.

Roll the dice to see who begins. The player with the lesser product plays first.

Take turns rolling the dice. Choose either the sum of the numbers you rolled, or just 1 of the numbers you rolled, and place it in one of the animals on your game sheet.

You must place a number on every turn, unless by placing the number you would be making an incorrect number sentence.

If you cannot place a number without making an incorrect number sentence, you lose that turn.

The first player to correctly complete all the number sentences is the winner.

VARIATIONS
Use 1 octahedron die.

As a solitaire game, complete as many of the number sentences as you can before you roll a number which cannot be used. Score 1 point for each sentence that you correctly completed.

GAME SHEET 22

NAME _____

BIG GAME HUNT

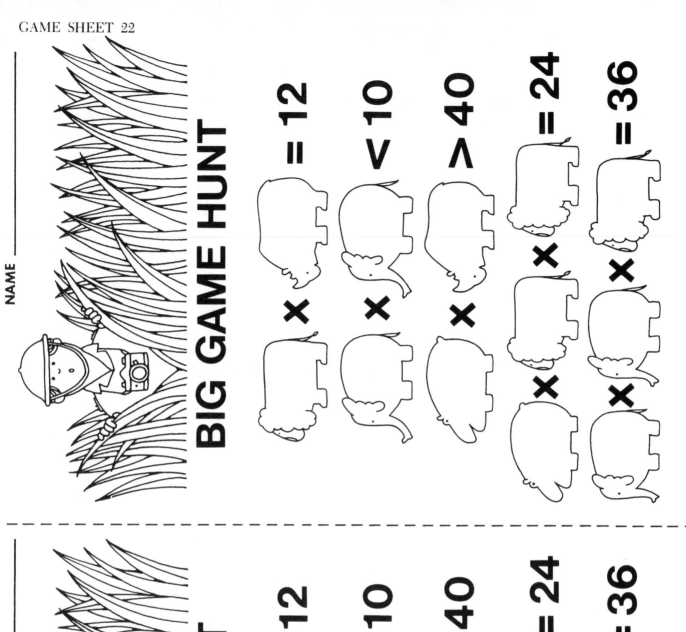

NAME _____

BIG GAME HUNT

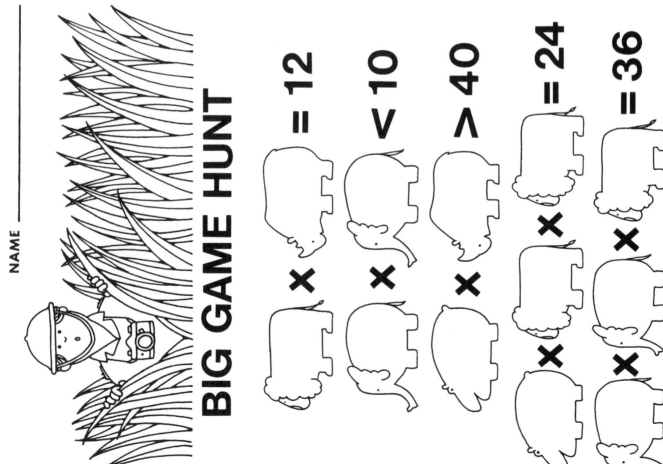

BLACK OUT

MATH SKILL
Basic division facts related to products through 36

NUMBER OF PLAYERS
2 to 4

MATERIALS

1 hexahedron die
Game sheet 23 (duplicate 1 sheet per player)
1 pencil per player

HOW TO PLAY
The object of the game is to black out as many windows as possible on your game sheet.

Each player rolls the die to determine who begins. The player with the lowest number plays first.

Take turns rolling the die. Black out 2 numbers whose quotient is the number you rolled, and state the division equation you used. For example, if you roll 3, you might black out 12 and 4, saying "$12 \div 4 = 3$," or you might black out 30 and 10, saying "$30 \div 10 = 3$."

Each number on your building may be blacked out only once.

If you roll a 1, you lose that turn.

If you state an incorrect division equation, you lose that turn.

Stop playing when you roll a number for which you cannot black out a pair of numbers.

When all players have reached the stopping point, count how many windows you blacked out.

The player with the most windows blacked out wins. In case of a tie, the player with the least sum of all numbers not blacked out is the winner.

VARIATION
The winner is the player with the least sum of numbers not blacked out after all players have stopped playing.

BLACK OUT

NAME

1	2	3
4	5	6
8	9	10
12	15	16
18	20	24
25	30	36

GAME 3 SCORE _____

1	2	3
4	5	6
8	9	10
12	15	16
18	20	24
25	30	36

GAME 2 SCORE _____

1	2	3
4	5	6
8	9	10
12	15	16
18	20	24
25	30	36

GAME 1 SCORE _____

QUOTE

MATH SKILL
Basic division facts related to products through 81

NUMBER OF PLAYERS
2 to 4

MATERIALS

1 icosahedron die
Game sheet 24
10 markers per player
Scissors

HOW TO PLAY
The object of the game is to get 4 markers in a row in any direction—horizontal, vertical, or diagonal.

Cut the QUOTE cards apart. Each player chooses 1 card for the first game.

The player whose first name begins with the letter closest to Z starts.

Take turns rolling the die. Cover 1 division problem on your card that has an answer equal to the number you rolled.

If your card does not have a division problem with an answer equal to the number you roll, or if you roll a zero, you lose that turn.

The first player to get 4 markers in a row in any direction is the winner.

Exchange QUOTE cards and play again in the same way.

VARIATION
The first player to cover the 4 corner spaces on the card is the winner.

QUOTE

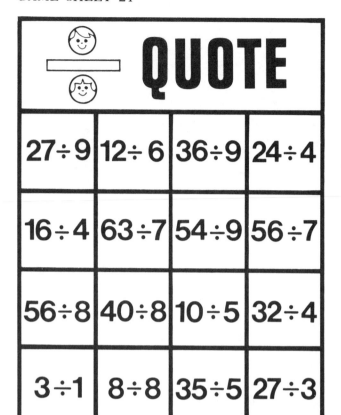

27÷9	12÷6	36÷9	24÷4
16÷4	63÷7	54÷9	56÷7
56÷8	40÷8	10÷5	32÷4
3÷1	8÷8	35÷5	27÷3

QUOTE

28÷7	14÷2	3÷3	72÷9
4÷2	54÷6	30÷5	45÷7
42÷6	18÷9	8÷2	7÷7
5÷1	24÷8	36÷6	35÷7

QUOTE

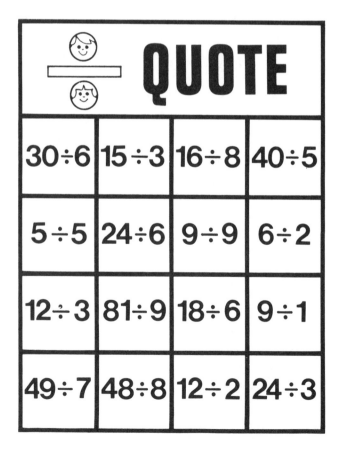

30÷6	15÷3	16÷8	40÷5
5÷5	24÷6	9÷9	6÷2
12÷3	81÷9	18÷6	9÷1
49÷7	48÷8	12÷2	24÷3

QUOTE

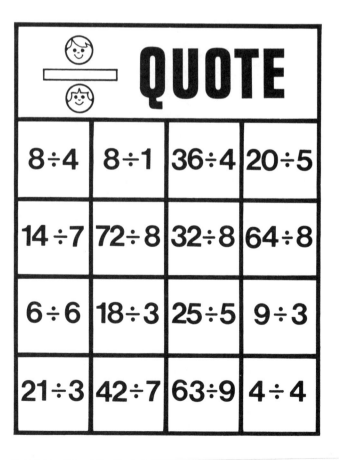

8÷4	8÷1	36÷4	20÷5
14÷7	72÷8	32÷8	64÷8
6÷6	18÷3	25÷5	9÷3
21÷3	42÷7	63÷9	4÷4

MOVING REMAINDERS

MATH SKILL
Division by 1-digit divisors (quotients with and without remainders)

NUMBER OF PLAYERS
2 to 5

MATERIALS

1 icosahedron die
Game sheet 25
1 marker per player

HOW TO PLAY
The object of the game is to reach *100*.

Roll the die to determine who begins. The player with the highest even number plays first.

All players begin with their markers on *11*.

Take turns rolling the die. Divide the number you rolled into the number your marker is on. Find the remainder in that division problem. Move your marker the number of spaces indicated by the remainder.

If the remainder is zero, you do not move.

If you roll a zero, move your marker back to the closest *TRUCK*, because division by zero is not allowed.

You may share a space with another player.

The first player to land on or pass *100* is the winner.

VARIATIONS
Use a dodecahedron, hexahedron (ordinary), or octahedron die.

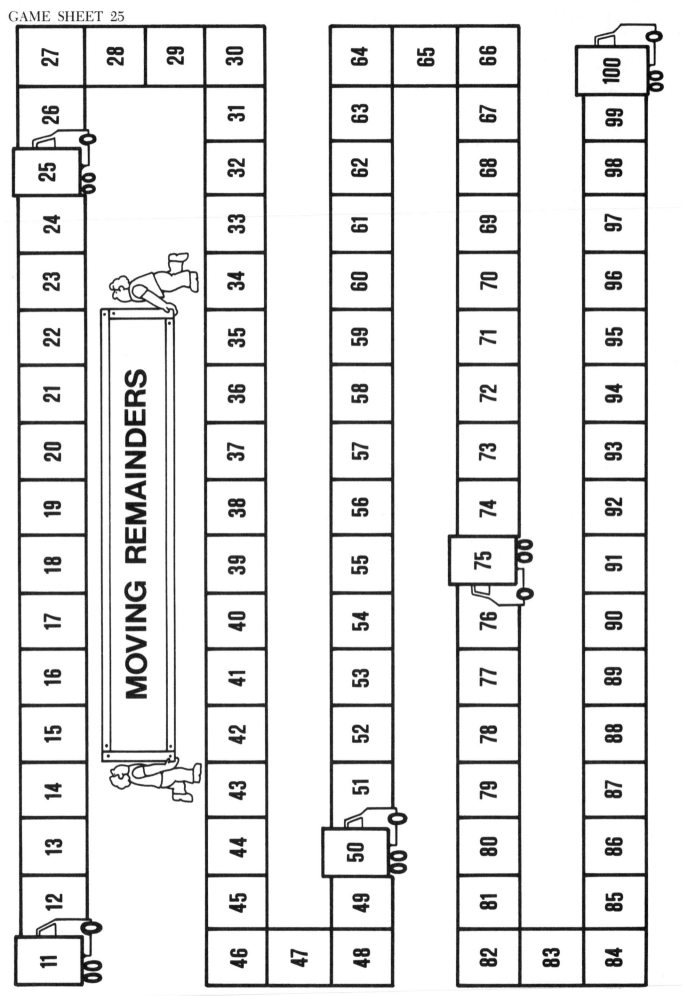

MOVING REMAINDERS

FIVE IN A ROW

MATH SKILLS
Addition facts through sums of 24
Adding or subtracting 1 from a number

NUMBER OF PLAYERS
2 to 5

MATERIALS

2 dodecahedra dice
Game sheet 26 (duplicate 1 sheet per player)
12 markers per player

HOW TO PLAY
The object of the game is to place 5 markers in a row in any direction—horizontal, vertical, or diagonal.

Each player rolls 1 die to see who begins. The player whose number is closest to 7 plays first.

Take turns rolling the dice. Find the sum of the numbers rolled. Add 1 to the sum, or subtract 1 from the sum, and cover the answer on your game sheet.

If you cannot cover an answer on your game sheet, you lose that turn.

The first player to place 5 markers in a row is the winner.

VARIATIONS
Change to 2, 3, 4, 5, or 6 the constant that is added or subtracted.

Use 2 icosahedra dice and add or subtract 6 from the sum.

5 in a ROW

1	2	3	4	5
6	7	8	9	10
11	12	13	14	15
16	17	18	19	20
21	22	23	24	25

BIGFOOT

MATH SKILL
  Basic addition and subtraction facts related to sums through 10

NUMBER OF PLAYERS
  2

MATERIALS

  2 hexahedra dice
  Game sheet 27
  1 marker per player

HOW TO PLAY
  The object of the game is to move your marker from *START* to *BIGFOOT* by finding sums or differences.

  Roll the dice to see who begins. Whoever rolls the greater sum starts, and chooses to play *TRACK 1* or *TRACK 2*. The other player plays the remaining track.

  Take turns rolling the dice. You may either add the 2 numbers you rolled, or subtract one number from the other. If that sum or difference is the next number on your track, you may move your marker to that number. If you cannot move, the other player may then add or subtract the same 2 numbers and try to move.

  Continue playing in the same way.

  To land on *BIGFOOT*, you or the other player must roll a double. (This means that if your marker is on the last space of your track and the other player rolls a double that he or she can't use, you may move your marker to *BIGFOOT*.

  The first player to land on *BIGFOOT* is the winner.

  NOTE: This game will take several minutes to play.

VARIATIONS
  Have the players use other polyhedra dice. Change the numbers on the tracks.

GAME SHEET 27

BIG FOOT

LEAP FROG

MATH SKILL

   Basic addition and subtraction facts related to sums through 18

NUMBER OF PLAYERS

   2

MATERIALS

   1 hexahedron die
   Game sheet 28
   1 marker per player

HOW TO PLAY

   The object of the game is to move your marker from your starting number to **9** by finding sums or differences.

   Roll the die to see who begins. Whoever rolls the higher number starts, and chooses to be Player 1 or Player 2. Player 1 starts on **0**. Player 2 starts on **18**.

   Take turns rolling the die. You may either add or subtract the number you rolled from the number you're on. For example, if you are on **12** and you roll a 6, you may move your marker to **6** (12 – 6) or to **18** (12 + 6).

   On each turn you *must* move your marker, but you may not move it off the number line. That means that sometimes you won't have a choice whether to add or to subtract.

   Continue playing until a player lands on **9**.

   The first player to land on **9** is the winner.

VARIATIONS

   Have the players use different polyhedra dice. Change the number on which they must land to win.

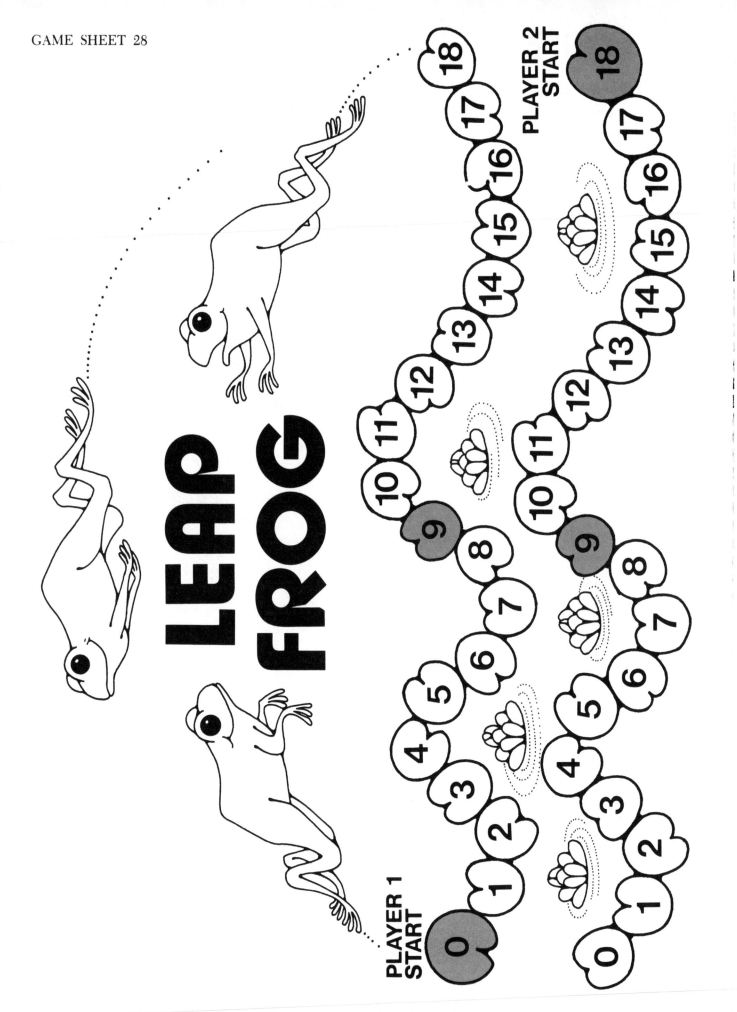

LEAP FROG

PLAYER 2 START

PLAYER 1 START

PYRAMID

MATH SKILLS
   Basic addition and subtraction facts for sums through 12
   Basic multiplication and division facts for products through 36

NUMBER OF PLAYERS
   2

MATERIALS

   2 hexahedra dice
   Game sheet 29
   2 colored pencils, crayons, or water-color markers

HOW TO PLAY
   The object of the game is to get the higher score.

   Each player rolls the dice to see who begins. The player with the greater product plays first.

   Take turns rolling the dice. Make a number by either adding, subtracting, multiplying, or dividing the 2 numbers rolled (answers may not have remainders). Shade in a space that has that answer in it.

   If the space you shade in is not next to any other shaded space, your score for that turn is zero.

   If the space you shade in is next to another shaded space, your score for that turn is the number in the space you shaded.

   If you cannot shade in any space, you lose that turn.

   The game ends when all the spaces have been shaded in or when each player has had 20 turns.

   Find your total score.

   The player with the higher total score is the winner.

   Example:

 Spaces that are next to each other

 or Spaces that are *not* next to each other

VARIATIONS
   The player with the lower total score is the winner.

   Have the player play this as a solitaire game. The player should attempt to score as many points as possible before getting 3 consecutive scores of zero.

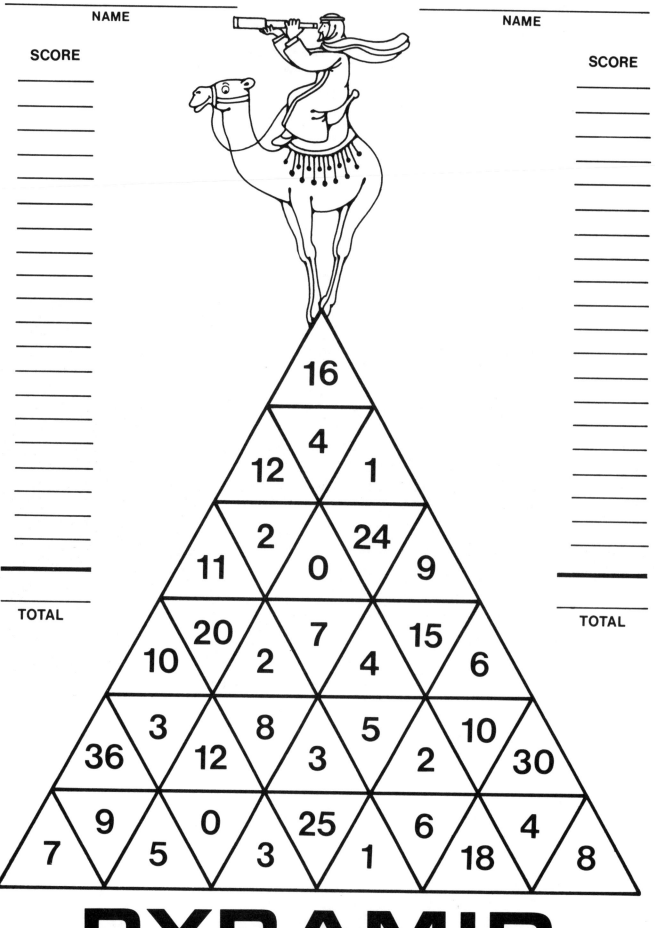

NAME

SCORE

TOTAL

NAME

SCORE

TOTAL

PYRAMID

POLYHEDRA DICE GAMES For Grades K to 6   © 1993 Ideal School Supply Company

100 IN THE SHADE

MATH SKILL
Basic addition, subtraction, multiplication, and division facts using the numbers
0 to 9

NUMBER OF PLAYERS
2 to 4

MATERIALS

2 icosahedra dice
Game sheet 30 (duplicate 1 per player)
Colored pencils, crayons, or water-color markers

HOW TO PLAY
The object of the game is to shade in all the spaces on your game sheet.

Roll the dice to see who begins. The player with the greatest product plays first.

Take turns rolling the dice. Use one of the operations—addition, subtraction, multiplication, or division—to combine the 2 numbers rolled. If you choose division, and the answer does not come out evenly, use the whole number part of the quotient and ignore any remainder. When you have the answer to the equation, shade in that number of spaces on your game sheet.

Write the equation you used on the game sheet, in the column marked *EQUATIONS*. For example, if you roll 5 and 6 and choose to multiply, write "5 × 6 = 30" and shade in 30 spaces.

If the 2 numbers rolled are such that you cannot make any answer from them that would equal the number of remaining unshaded spaces, you lose that turn.

You must use each of the 4 basic operations once during the first 4 turns of the game. After that, you may use any operation you choose on any turn.

The first player to shade in all the spaces *exactly* is the winner.

VARIATIONS
Use a grid of 200 squares.

Any operation may be used on any turn, but the same operation may not be used on 2 successive turns.

100
IN THE
SHADE

EQUATIONS

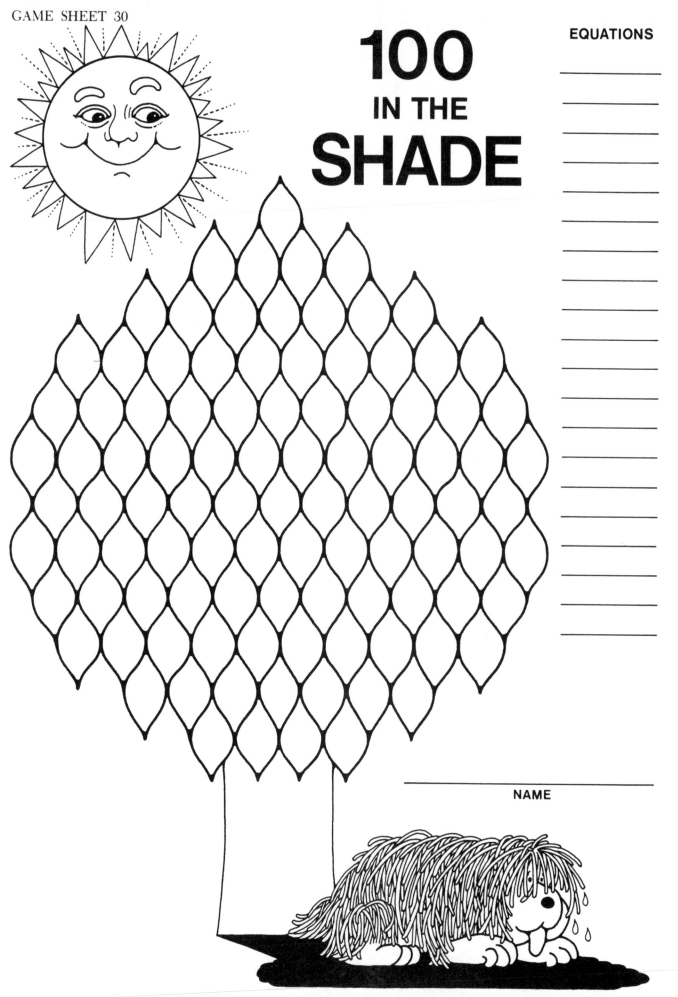

_____

NAME

PUTT PUTT

MATH SKILL
Basic addition, subtraction, multiplication, and division facts using the numbers 1 through 12

NUMBER OF PLAYERS
2 to 5

MATERIALS

2 dodecahedra dice
Game sheet 31
Pencil

HOW TO PLAY
The object of the game is to get the lowest score at the end of 9 holes of play.

Roll the dice to see who begins. The player with the least product plays first.

Read the rule for the hole you are playing. Each player in turn rolls the dice as many times as necessary (up to a maximum of 7 rolls) to satisfy the rules of the hole. Your score for a particular hole is the number of times you rolled the dice to satisfy the rules. For example, if Player 1 is rolling for *HOLE 1*, and the numbers rolled are (4,7), (6,6), (5,11), and (7,1), Player 1's score for *HOLE 1* is 4, because he or she satisfied the rule of the hole on the fourth toss of the dice.

If you roll the dice 7 times without satisfying the rule of the hole, score 7 for the hole and pass the dice to the next player.

The player with the lowest total score at the end of 9 holes of play is the winner.

VARIATIONS
As a solitaire game, have the player play the 9 holes 3 times and determine the lowest score for the 3 rounds.

Change the rules of the holes to provide easier or more difficult problems.

Name _____

SCORECARD*

PUTT PUTT

HOLE	PLAYER 1	PLAYER 2	PLAYER 3	PLAYER 4	PLAYER 5	RULE FOR HOLE
1						A one is rolled.
2						Sum is divisible by 2.
3						Product is odd .
4						Sum > 9.
5						Sum is a multiple of 3.
6						Product > 100.
7						Difference < 3.
8						Sum = 7.
9						Quotient is a whole number.
TOTAL						

* Score is the number of rolls needed to satisfy the rule for the hole. Maximum score for any hole is 7.

BEE LINE

MATH SKILLS

Combining 3 numbers using addition, subtraction, and multiplication
Using the distributive property of multiplication over addition or subtraction

NUMBER OF PLAYERS

2 or 3

MATERIALS

3 hexahedra dice
Game sheet 32
20 colored markers per player (2 cm squares of construction paper, or small chips)

HOW TO PLAY

The object of the game is to place 4 of your markers in a row—horizontally or diagonally.

Each player chooses a set of colored markers.

Each player rolls the 3 dice to see who begins. The player with the least sum plays first.

Take turns rolling the dice. Use 1 or 2 operations (addition, subtraction, or multiplication) on the 3 numbers rolled. Place one of your markers on your answer and state how you got your answer. For example, if 2, 4, and 1 are rolled, some possible answers would be: $7 = 2 + 4 + 1$; $8 = 2 \times 4 \times 1$; $1 = 4 - 2 - 1$; $10 = 2 (4 + 1)$; $6 = 2(4 - 1)$; $2 = 1(4 - 2)$; $12 = 4(2 + 1)$.

If you cannot make an answer for any of the numbers left uncovered, you lose that turn.

If you state an incorrect answer, you lose that turn.

If a player passes the dice stating that there is no answer he or she can cover, but you see a way that a correct answer could be made, call out the mistake and place your marker on that answer.

The first player to get 4 of his or her own markers in a row is the winner.

VARIATION

After 1 marker is on the board, a player may only place a marker on an answer which is next to another covered space. After each player has had 10 turns, the player with the most markers on the board is the winner.

Example:

Spaces that are next to each other

Spaces that are *not* next to each other

POLYHEDRA DICE GAMES For Grades K to 6   © 1993 Ideal School Supply Company

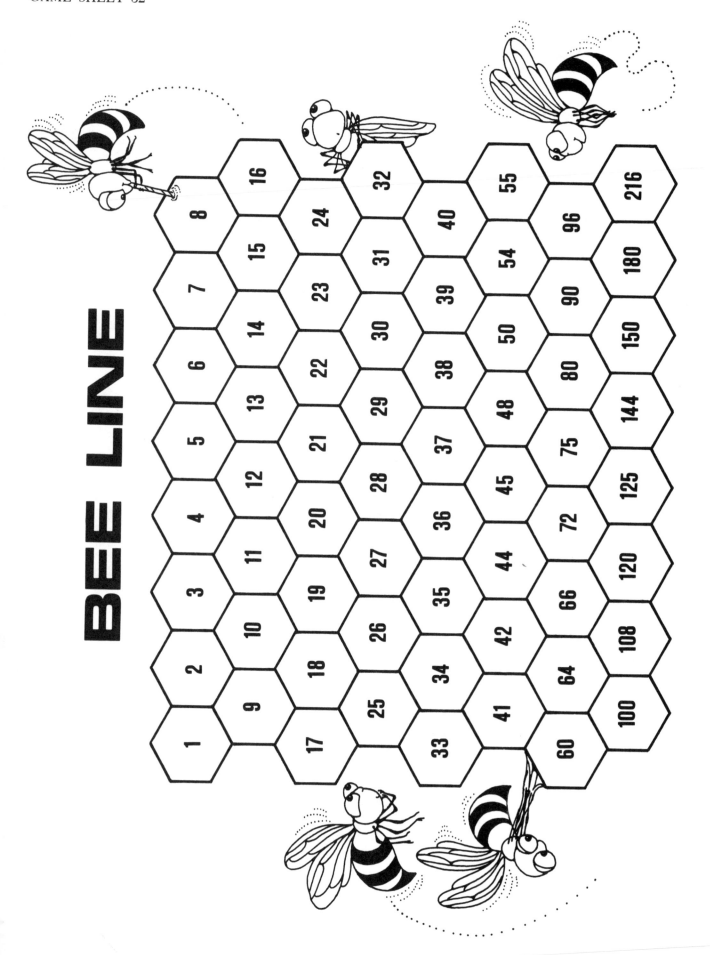

BEE LINE

FRACTION MAGIC

MATH SKILL
  Reducing fractions to lowest terms

NUMBER OF PLAYERS
  2 to 5

MATERIALS

  2 octahedra dice
  Game sheet 33 (duplicate 1 sheet per player)
  20 markers per player

HOW TO PLAY
  The object of the game is to get 4 markers in a row in any direction—horizontal, vertical, or diagonal.

  Roll the dice to see who begins. Whoever can form the greatest fraction less than 1 plays first.

  Take turns rolling the dice. Using one number as the numerator and the other number as the denominator, form a fraction less than or equal to 1. Place a marker on a fraction that is equivalent to the one you made.

  For example, if you roll 6 and 4, the fraction you make is $\frac{4}{6}$. You reduce this fraction to $\frac{2}{3}$, and place a marker on the space numbered $\frac{2}{3}$ on your game sheet. If you roll 5 and 5, the fraction you make is $\frac{5}{5}$, which reduces to 1. You place a marker on a space numbered 1 on your game sheet.

  If you roll a fraction that is no longer uncovered on the game board, you lose that turn.

  The first player to get 4 markers in a row in any direction is the winner.

VARIATION
  Two or 3 players use 1 game sheet and 2 or 3 sets of colored markers. Follow the same rules of play. The first player to get 3 markers in a row is the winner. Blocking strategies become an important part of this game.

$\dfrac{1}{4}$ $\dfrac{1}{4}$ $\dfrac{1}{2}$

FRACTION MAGIC

1	$\dfrac{1}{8}$	$\dfrac{1}{4}$	$\dfrac{3}{8}$	$\dfrac{1}{2}$	$\dfrac{5}{8}$
$\dfrac{3}{4}$	$\dfrac{7}{8}$	1	$\dfrac{1}{7}$	$\dfrac{2}{7}$	$\dfrac{3}{7}$
$\dfrac{4}{7}$	$\dfrac{5}{7}$	$\dfrac{6}{7}$	1	$\dfrac{1}{6}$	$\dfrac{1}{3}$
$\dfrac{1}{2}$	$\dfrac{2}{3}$	$\dfrac{5}{6}$	1	$\dfrac{1}{5}$	$\dfrac{2}{5}$
$\dfrac{3}{5}$	$\dfrac{4}{5}$	1	$\dfrac{1}{4}$	$\dfrac{1}{2}$	$\dfrac{3}{4}$
1	$\dfrac{1}{3}$	$\dfrac{2}{3}$	1	$\dfrac{1}{2}$	1

TOURNAMENT

MATH SKILL
  Ordering decimals

NUMBER OF PLAYERS
  A class or small group

MATERIALS

  1 icosahedron die
  Game sheet 34 (duplicate 1 game sheet per player)
  1 pencil per player

HOW TO PLAY
  The object of the game is to make the greatest decimal number.

  The teacher (or a student designated by the teacher) rolls the die.

  You place the number rolled in one of the 3 boxes (that is, in the tenths', hundredths', or thousandths' place) in row A. The teacher rolls the die a second time and you place the number in one of the 2 remaining boxes in row A. The teacher rolls the die a third time, and you place the number in the empty box in row A.

  The teacher will continue rolling the die until all the rows have been filled with 3-digit decimals.

  Determine the decimals in the *QUARTERFINALS*, the *SEMIFINALS*, and finally the *CHAMP*. Compare the decimals within each bracket, and choose the greater of the 2 decimals you are comparing. Write the greater of the 2 decimals on the line to the right, until you find the *CHAMP*. For example, the greater of the 2 decimals in rows A and B will be the first decimal in the *QUARTERFINALS*.

  The player with the greatest *CHAMP* is the winner.

VARIATION
  Compare the decimals and choose the lesser of the 2 decimals. The player with the least *CHAMP* is the winner.

NAME

TOURNAMENT

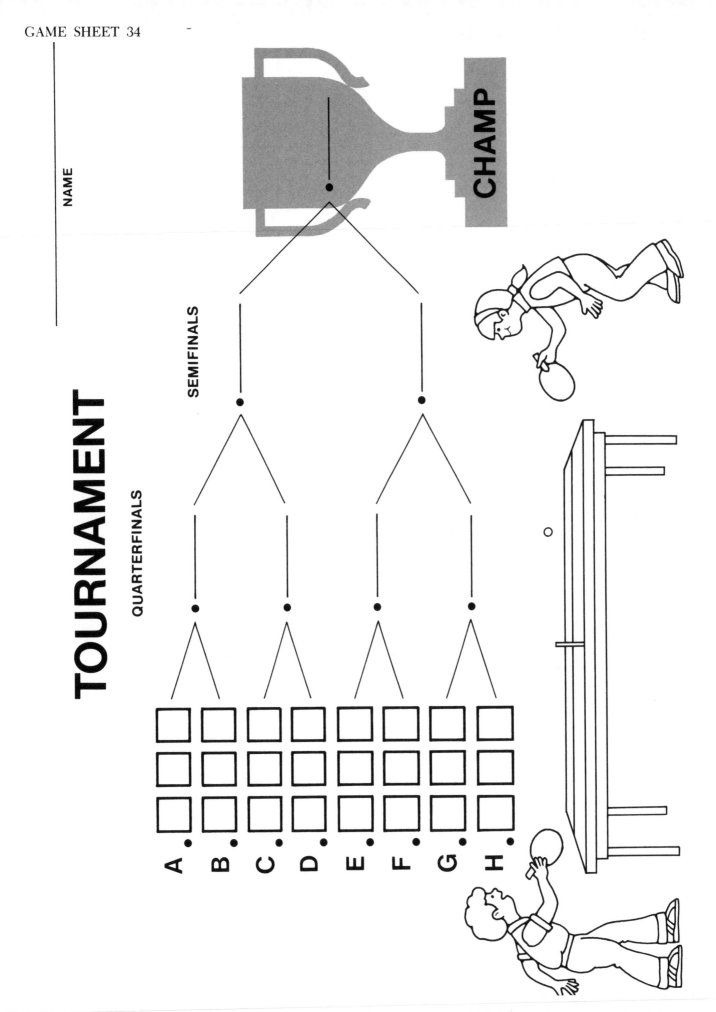

CHAMP

SEMIFINALS

QUARTERFINALS

A.
B.
C.
D.
E.
F.
G.
H.

DECIMAL RALLY

MATH SKILL
Addition, subtraction, multiplication, and division of decimals

NUMBER OF PLAYERS
A class or small group

MATERIALS

1 icosahedron die
Game sheet 35 (duplicate 1 half-sheet per player)
1 pencil per player

HOW TO PLAY
The object of the game is to make the greatest total decimal number.

The teacher (or a student designated by the teacher) rolls the die and calls out the number rolled. You place the number in any one of the 8 cars on your game sheet. The teacher will continue to roll the die for a total of 8 times. Each time, place the number in one of the cars.

There are 2 special rules:
In row B, you must place numbers which allow you to subtract a smaller number from a larger number, or your answer to that row will be zero.
In row D, you may not place a zero in the second car, because division by zero is undefined. If you place a zero in the second car, you are automatically disqualified from the game.

After all the 8 cars have been filled, perform the operation indicated for each row, and write your answers in the flags. Round the answer in row D to the nearest hundredth.

Add all the decimal numbers in the flags together to find the total.

The player with the greatest total decimal number is the winner.

VARIATION
The player with the least total decimal number is the winner. In this variation, if the subtraction in row B cannot be performed, your answer to row B is automatically 1.

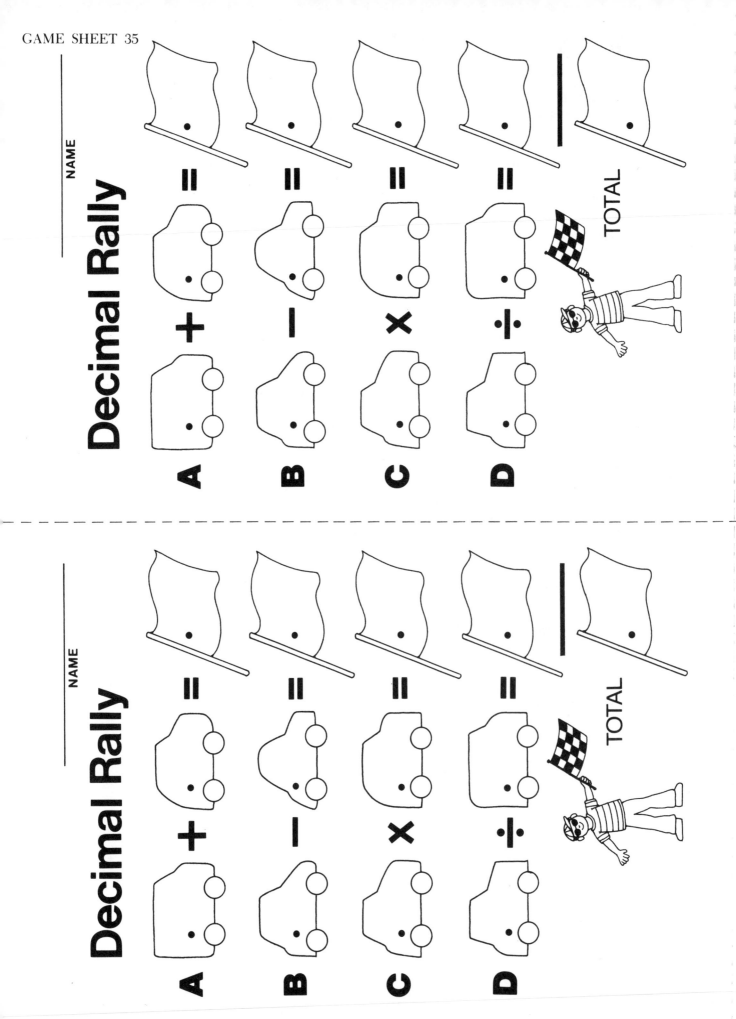

Decimal Rally

A ⊓ + ⊓ = ⊓

B ⊓ − ⊓ = ⊓

C ⊓ × ⊓ = ⊓

D ⊓ ÷ ⊓ = ⊓

TOTAL

POLYHEDRA DICE GAMES For Grades K to 6   © 1993 Ideal School Supply Company

SHAPES

MATH SKILL
  Identifying geometric shapes

NUMBER OF PLAYERS
  2 to 4

MATERIALS

  1 tetrahedron die
  Game sheet 36
  1 marker per player

HOW TO PLAY
  The object of the game is to land on the last shape on the game board.

  The player whose last name contains the most letters plays first.

  Take turns rolling the die. Move your marker the number of spaces shown on the die.
  If you can name the shape in the space you land on, you may keep your marker there.
  If you cannot name the shape, you must return your marker to its previous position.

  The names of the figures are:

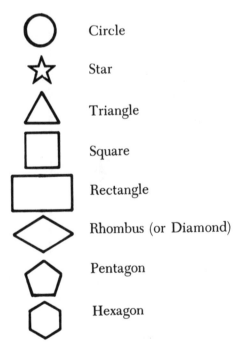

  The first player to land exactly on the last shape is the winner.

VARIATION
  Name the star and circle, and count the number of sides in the other shapes.

TURTLE RACE

MATH SKILL
Measuring in centimeters

NUMBER OF PLAYERS
2 to 4

MATERIALS

1 octahedron die
Game sheet 37
1 or more centimeter rulers
Pencils

HOW TO PLAY
The object of the game is to reach the *FINISH* line.

Each player rolls the die to see who begins. The player with the lowest number plays first, and races in *LANE 1*.

Take turns rolling the die. Put the centimeter ruler by your lane, with the zero mark at the *START* line. Measure off the number of centimeters shown by the die, and place a mark at that spot on your lane. On your next turn, place the zero mark of the ruler at the last mark you put on your lane.

The first player to touch or cross the *FINISH* line is the winner.

VARIATIONS
Use a tetrahedron die or a hexahedron (ordinary) die.

GAME SHEET 37

ISLAND HOP

MATH SKILL
   Measuring in centimeters

NUMBER OF PLAYERS
   2 to 4

MATERIALS

   1 dodecahedron die
   Game sheet 38 (duplicate 1 sheet per player)
   1 centimeter ruler per player
   1 pencil per player

HOW TO PLAY
   The object of the game is to land on every island.

   Each player rolls the die to see who begins. The player who rolls the highest number
   plays first.

   Take turns rolling the die. Use your centimeter ruler to draw a line as many
   centimeters long as the number you rolled. Begin the first segment at the tip of the
   seagull's beak. Begin all the other segments at the point where your last segment
   stopped.

   To land on an island, you must draw a segment that stops at a point inside the island.
   When you have landed on an island, shade it in. You may not draw a segment across
   an island unless that segment allows you to land on the island.

   You must draw a segment on every turn.

   The first player to land on all 6 islands is the winner.

VARIATIONS
   Use a dodecahedron die to indicate the number of centimeters and an icosahedron
   die to indicate the number of millimeters. Draw line segments to the appropriate
   length in centimeters and millimeters.

NAME

island hop

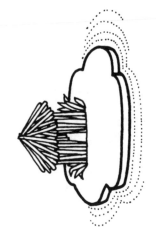

RAT RACE

MATH SKILLS
Identifying directions on a coordinate graph
Counting spaces on a coordinate graph

NUMBER OF PLAYERS
2 to 4

MATERIALS

1 tetrahedron die
Game sheet 39
1 marker per player

HOW TO PLAY
The object of the game is to reach the *CHEESE* at the point (9,9).

Each player rolls the die to see who begins. The player who rolls the lowest number plays first.

All markers begin at the *RAT*, point (0,0).

Take turns rolling the die twice. The first number you roll tells you how many spaces you should move your marker horizontally to the right. The second number tells you how many spaces to move your marker vertically up. When you have finished moving your marker, if you have landed on a *CAT* or a *TRAP*, move your marker back to (0,0).

Once your marker lands inside the shaded area, you only roll the die once for your turn. You may move your marker either up or to the right, moving your marker the number of spaces shown on the die.

If the number(s) you roll would make your marker move off the game board, you lose that turn.

The first player to reach the *CHEESE* is the winner.

VARIATION
Roll 2 tetrahedra dice and use either number to indicate how many points you move to the right and up. For example, if you roll 4 and 2, you may move right 4 and up 2, or right 2 and up 4.

RAT RACE

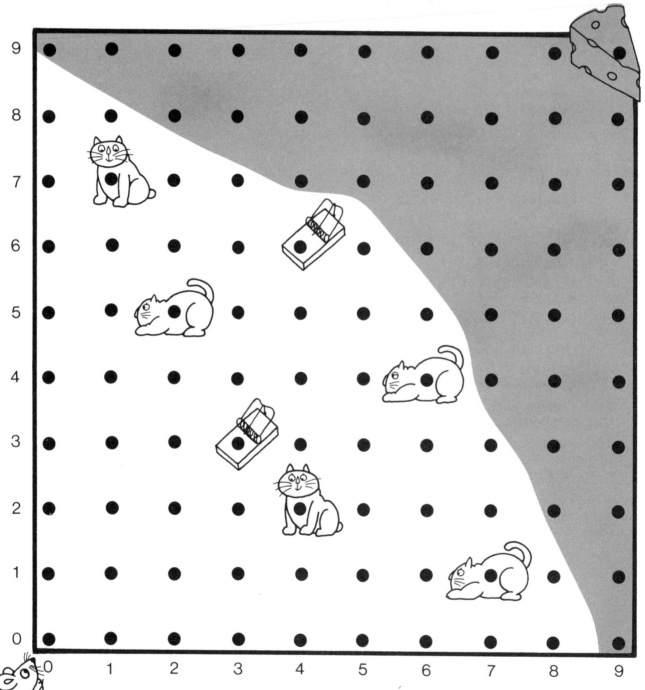

ZEBRA STRIPES

MATH SKILL
Locating points on a coordinate graph

NUMBER OF PLAYERS
2

MATERIALS

2 octahedra dice
Game sheet 40
2 pencils

HOW TO PLAY
The object of the game is to get 3 marks in a row in any direction—horizontal, vertical, or diagonal.

Each player rolls the dice to see who begins. The player who rolls the greater sum plays first, and uses a mark of "X". The other player uses a mark of "O".
Take turns rolling the dice. The 2 numbers you roll represent the coordinates of a point on the graph. For example, if you roll 4 and 7, you may choose the point (4,7) or the point (7,4). Place your mark (X or O) over the point you choose from the 2 numbers you roll.

If you roll numbers for which all the points have already been marked, roll again.

The first player to get 3 of his or her own marks in a row in any direction is the winner.

VARIATION
Use 3 octahedra dice. Choose any 2 of the numbers you roll to pick a point to mark. The first player to place 4 of his or her own marks in a row in any direction is the winner.

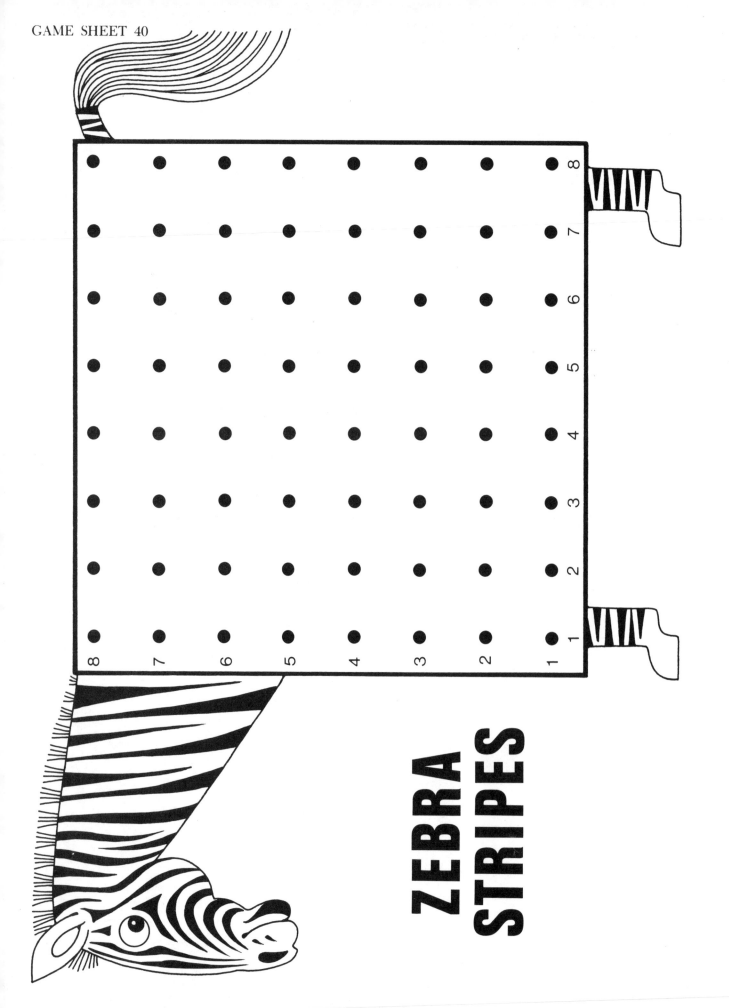

ZEBRA STRIPES